To Thea, on your 1ot &
From Nana & Papa

Miraculous Me

STORY BY
RUTH PENDERGAST SISSEL

ILLUSTRATIONS BY
TINA TOLLIVER MATNEY

Presented with Love

to _____

from _____

MIRACULOUS ME

Published by Caritas Press
P.O. Box 2452
Gilbert, AZ 85299

Printed in the USA

First Edition
10 9 8 7 6 5 4 3 2 1
ISBN 978-1-940209-04-3

For Re-orders: MiraculousMeBook@gmail.com

Acknowledgements

To my parents, whose love and unwavering support have created innumerable opportunities throughout my life. To my husband, Mike, thank you for your loving encouragement and for being my greatest cheerleader! To my daughters Emerson and Ivy, thank you for filling my heart with beautiful inspiration. To my cherished family and friends on earth and in heaven, your spirit moves me. To my Beloved Grandma, Lucia Belle Rowland, your love, prayers and gift of poetry have inspired generations. Most of all, to my Heavenly Father who softly whispered these words to my heart.

A special thanks to my sweet partners on this journey, the incredibly talented artist, Tina Tolliver Matney, who gave life to my words; and Sherry Boas, editor and publisher extraordinaire, for her loving belief and support of this little book with a lot of heart.

--Ruth Pendergast Sissel

RUTH PENDERGAST SISSEL is an author, entrepreneur and mom who has always been passionate about journal writing and poetry. When she was a small child, God placed a dream in her heart to one day publish a children's book. In 2007, pregnant with her first child, she often found herself in deep reflection about the miracle of life. Looking back, it is clear to her that Christ was beginning to breathe life into her dream of writing a children's book. In early spring 2013, while putting socks on her newest daughter's feet, Ruth spoke out loud, "Look at those toes, where will they go?" In a moment of sheer inspiration, she grabbed her eldest daughter's Tinkerbell notebook, and between folding laundry and scrambling eggs, wrote the manuscript for this book. Ruth lives in Chandler, Arizona, with her two daughters, Emerson and Ivy, and her husband Mike.

For Jillian, Isabelle, Oliver, Daemon, Carter and Lucas. You are my joy and my inspiration.

--Tina Tolliver Matney

For my daughters, Emerson & Ivy, who fill my heart with love and inspiration.

--Ruth Pendergast Sissel

After spending several years instructing art and coordinating school art programs, **TINA TOLLIVER MATNEY** decided it was time to pursue her dream of becoming an illustrator of children's books. Much of her time is spent in her art studio, but she also keeps busy with family who live nearby. She lives on the Kettle River in Washington and has a love for gardening and a passion for wildlife rescue.

Mommy and Daddy
are on their way.
They won't soon forget
this glorious day.

They are about to be given the chance to see
The hidden miracle I call "me."

A twisting tornado
of life and love,
A perfect creation,
a gift from above.
Before I breathe,
I am already a treasure.
God knows me
and loves me
beyond all measure.

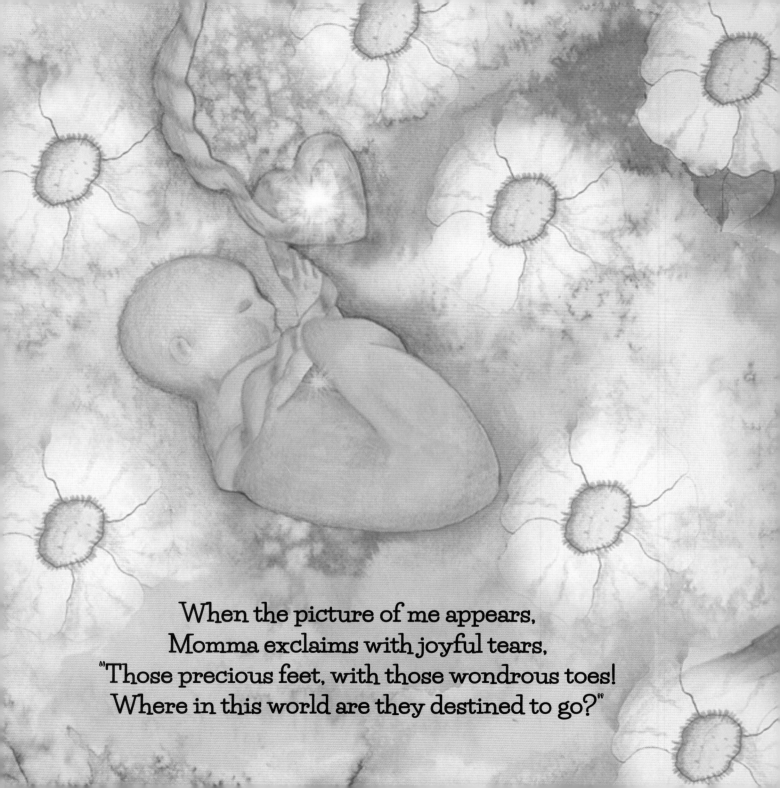

When the picture of me appears,
Momma exclaims with joyful tears,
"Those precious feet, with those wondrous toes!
Where in this world are they destined to go?"

Daddy says, "Look at those fingers! What perfect design! I can't wait 'til they are wrapped around mine."

Adventures await, as dreams unfold.
What will those precious hands hold?
My finger with the first step you take...

A small silver whisk helping
Mommy to bake,

Maybe a drum,
pounding a beat.

And where will you dash
with those tiny feet?

Will they carry you fast
over dew-wet grass?

Or splash in waters
once still as glass?

Will you climb giant mountains?
Explore distant lands?
Build intricate castles from grains of sand?

What wonders will your eyes behold?
What blessings will your life unfold?

Will you make music
the world has
never heard?

Will you fly like a jet
and soar like a bird?

A statuesque ballerina
with unwavering grace,

Maybe an astronaut
zooming through space,

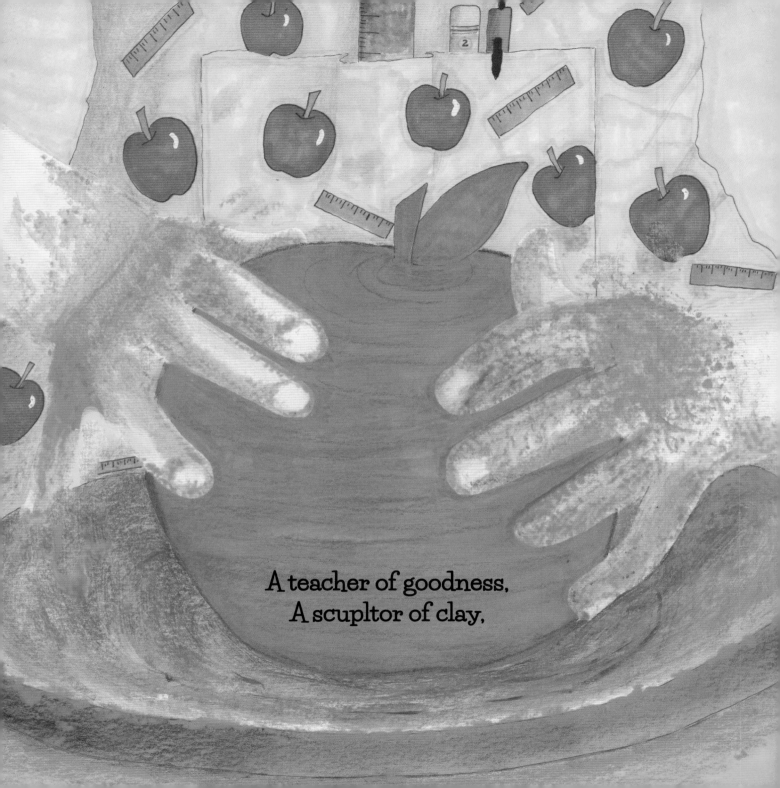

A teacher of goodness,
A scupltor of clay,

Maybe a farmer
tending your hay,

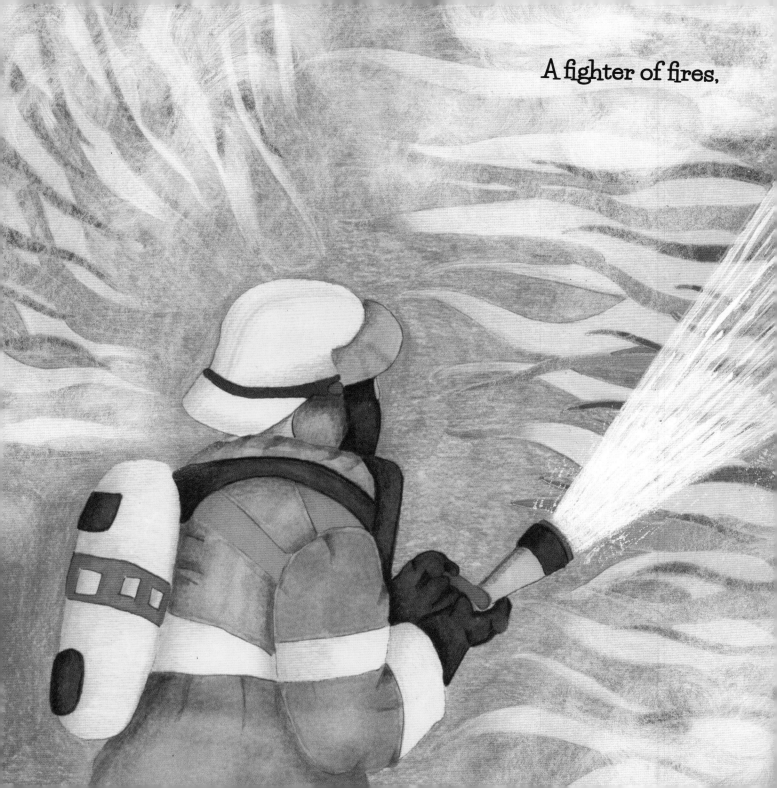

A fighter of fires,

A surfer of waves,

A weaver of fabrics,

A pastor who saves.

Will you stand at attention,
so brave and strong?

Or hold your own tiny baby
and whisper a song?

Wherever life takes you,
whatever it holds,
remember these words.
They're more precious than gold:
You were knitted together and
wonderfully made,
with God's perfect Love
lighting your way,

Guiding your footsteps
and holding you tight,

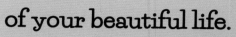

of your beautiful life.

and the highers

Through the highs